TENNESSEE

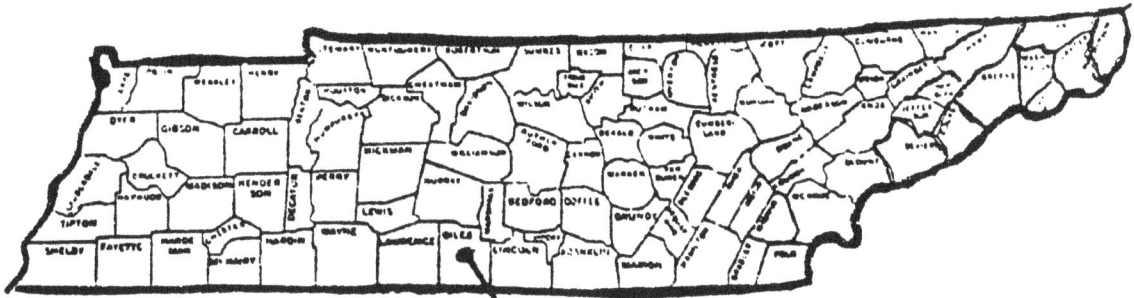

Giles County

Marriages

1818 - 1862

by

ERMA LEE BROWN

1978

Originally Published:

Byron Sistler and Associates, Inc.
Nashville, Tennessee
1978

Reprinted for
Byron Sistler and Associates, Inc.

by

Janaway Publishing, Inc.
732 Kelsey Ct.
Santa Maria, California 93454
(805) 925-1038
www.JanawayGenealogy.com

2013

ISBN: 978-1-59641-131-9

GILES COUNTY TENNESSEE MARRIAGES
1818 ----------- 1862

GROOM	BRIDE	DATE	OFFICIAL OR SECURITY
Mason, Isaac	Edwards, Nancy	17 Nov 1818	unsigned
Edwards, John	Burch, Mary C.	4 Feb 1822	Joshua Butcher,
Shockley, Benj.(x)	Beale, Lilly	23 Nov 1822	Wm. Swinney (x), Sec.
Brown, Beverly	Abernathy, Adaline	27 Mar 1823	H.H. Brown
Melton, Henry	Brooks, Joanna	30 Mar 1824	Milton Hill, MG
Ogilby, Edward H.	Vassar, Martha	20 Jul 1824	Anderson Hogan, JP
Davidson, Butler	Brownlow, Elizabeth	15 May 1826	George M. Gibson, Sec.
Brown, William R.	Smith, Abigail	31 Jan 1827	Ira E. Brown, Sec.
Owens, Lee H.	Lumbach, Sally	3 Jan 1831	Buckner Maddry(x), Sec.
Taylor, James	Taylor, Mary	1 Mar 1831	Jacob Jones, JP
Conoly, Archibald	Price, Mary S.A.	31 July 1832	Elias Tidwell, JP
Davenport, Matthew	Hopkins, Sarah B.	1 Aug 1832	Allen Hill,
Ingram, Isaac	Bradley, Mary Ann	28 Oct 1832	David Crook,
Hargrove, William A.	Rhea, Hannah	1 Nov 1832	David I. Moore, JP
King, Griffin L.	Burrow, Nancy H.	21 Sep 1833	Martin S. Jones, Sec
Taylor, James H.	Philips, Lucy Ann	3 Jan 1837	Jacob Jones,
Todd, Presley N.	Hammons, Matilda	12 Jan 1837	James White, JP
Davis, William	Harrison, Mary Ann	4 Mar 1837	James Harrison, Sec.
Beaver, Lemuel	Moore, Belinda	20 Mar 1837	Robert Neal, JP
Gladish, Joshua B.	Briggs, Maria A.	13 Apr 1837	Irvin R. Brown, Sec.
Tillery, Charles M.	Apperson, Lucy S.	4 May 1837	G. D. Taylor,
Jones, Henry	Sherwood, Anna	20 Aug 1837	Jacob Jones, JP
Bryan, John W.	France, Martha	16 Dec 1937	J.M. Busick, JP
Moore, James	McMillian, Maria	28 Dec 1837	G. Vansant,
Erwin, James G.	West, Marilla	27 Dec 1837	E.D. Jones, Sec.
Graham, James P.	Dickey, Margarett	21 June 1838	James Gaines,
Davidson, George W.	Dodson, Lydia Jane	17 Sep 1838	no return
Wright, Newton E.	Lester, Minerva T.	28 Nov 1838	Joseph B. Moore, Sec.
Laird, Samuel R.	Seamour, Martha Catharine	8 Aug 1839	George F. Phelps, Sec. David Crook,
Huff, Wiley	McCallum, Sarah	25 Jun 1840	Geo.F. Phelps, Sec E.McMillian, VDM
Patterson, Simpson A.	Shadden, Amanda M.	10 Jan 1841	P.H. Ezell, Sec. H.H. Brown, EME
Castleberry, Franklin	Hackney, Eveline Tennessee	13 Jan 1841	Richard Abernathy, JP

GILES COUNTY TENNESSEE MARRIAGES

GROOM	BRIDE	DATE	OFFICIAL OR SECURITY
Curtis, Isaiah also as	Barr, Nancy Doyle, Nancy	24 Mar 1841	Philip Manuel, Sec Nehemiah Howard, JP
Nicholas, Thomas (x)	Brookshire, Minerva G.	4 Jun 1841	Josiah Brookshire, Sec.
Barnes, George W.	Luker, Ella Jane	31 Aug 1841	Jesse Luker, JP
Gardner, George W.	Ezell, Caroline F.	18 Oct 1841	Homer R. Jones, Sec. Jesse Westmoreland, JP
Green, Robert	Collins, Maria	14 Oct 1841	J.K. White, JP
Arthur, Henry D.	Riggs, Geney (lic-Jency)	28 Oct 1841	John Hughes, Sec. Warren W. Calhoun, JP
Shrader, Daniel G.	Angus, Mary T.	16 Oct 1841	F.T. McLaurine, JP
Barnes, Uriah E.	Tacker, Elizabeth	25 Jan 1842	James C. Shores, Sec. M.V. Luna, JP
Nave, Jacob	Stone, Jane	6 Jan 1843	Jehu Nave, JP
Yarbrough, David	Woodward, Elizabeth	14 Feb 1843	Jesse Westmoreland, JP
Williams, Robert	Harwell, Ladocea Ann	11 May 1843	Jesse Westmoreland, JP
Jones, John L.	Hanna, Martha A.	26 Oct 1843	William Inman, JP
Burnett, Thomas M.	Whitfield, Mary J.	4 Dec 1843	James H. Strong, Sec.
Erwin, Robert W.	Jane E. Woods	12 Dec 1843	H.B. Warren, MG
Curry, Alfred	White, Mary	16 Jan 1844	William M. Clark(x), Sec.
Clanton, William T.	Robertson, Bethana	13 Jun 1844	Hezekiah, Jackson, Sec.
Whitt, Ephriam D.	Smith, Sarah	6 Jul 1844	Isaac Whitt, Sec.
Winn, Minor H.	Patrick, Jane M.	19 Aug 1844	Major A. Kennedy, Sec.
Shadden, Elisha M.	Ramsey, Olivia Ann	1 Oct 1844	William T. Well, MG
Orr, Thomas W.	Walker, Mary A.	24 Oct 1844	Henry Miller,
Simms, Robert H.	Carter, Nancy	13 Dec 1844	William Levesque, EME
Jackson, John B.	Litterall, Jerusia Ann	1 Jan 1845	faded-unreadable
Murrell, William	Hillhouse, Mary Caroline	25 Mar 1845	James W. Curtis, Sec.
Graham, Alexander	Tucker, Violet	18 Mar 1846	William Perry, JP
Vaughan, David	Dickerson, Cynthia B.	17 May 1846	Nicholas C. Buford, JP
Freeman, Joel E.	Wilson, Louisa M.	2 Jul 1846	A. M. Pickens, MG
Oliver, William H.	Wilson, Sarah A.	21 Jul 1846	Ira E. Brown, JP
Dunn, William D.	Neal, Ann Henry	6 Aug 1846	Robert Caldwell, VDM
Erwin, James	Frazier, Julia	12 Aug 1846	G.D. Taylor,
Smith, Henry W.	Farmer, Nancy A.	15 Sep 1846	unsigned
Potts, George H.	Garrett, Elizabeth B.	29 Sep 1846	Ira E. Brown, JP
Craig, William B.	Gordon, Elizabeth	26 Nov 1846	Jehu Nave, JP

GILES COUNTY TENNESSEE MARRIAGES

GROOM	BRIDE	DATE	OFFICIAL OR SECURITY
Wilson, Andrew W.	McCallum, Xantippe L.	8 Dec 1846	A.M. Pickens, MG
Hood, Sterling C.	Vinson, Sarah Jane	15 Dec 1846	William Levesque, EME
Waller, Joseph C.	Carter, Eliza Jane	7 Sep 1848	Carson R. West, Sec.
Reid, James B.	Stratton, Mary C.	24 Sep 1849	E. Patrick Massey, Sec.
Stewart, William	Devasier, Minerva Caroline	24 Sep 1849	James Carrell, Sec.
Daggett, Miller	Moore, Cynthia Jane	25 Sep 1849	Samuel R. Foust, Sec.
Johnston, James T.	Rainey, Mahala A.	27 Sep 1849	Joseph B. Stamps, Sec.
Beckham, William J.	Booth, Therra	2 Oct 1849	Thomas W. Peterson, Sec
Dodson, John M.(x)	Powers, Nancy M.	3 Oct 1849	Robert B. Powers (x), S
McEwen, John	Johnston, Susannah Jane	8 Oct 1849	Copeland Whitfield, Sec
Kincaid, William C.	McMullen, Eliza Ellen	13 Oct 1849	Sam S. Farmer, Sec.
Fuller, Caid (x)	Garrett, Sarah	23 Oct 1849	John Fuller (x), Sec.
McCormack, Reuben M.	Brown, Mary E.	26 Oct 1849	J.H. Birdsong,
Follis, William R.	Myres, Eliza	14 Nov 1849	W.C. Moore,
Lucy, Ferdinand P.	Briggs, Frances S.	29 Dec 1849	T.M. Harwell, MG
Burgess, John	Gardner, Jane	8 Jan 1859	J.W. Lee, MG
Smith, Almus H.	Tarpley, Susannah	15 Jan 1850	Jeff Birdsong,
Kimbrough, Romulus S.	Kimbrough, Mary E.	31 Jan 1850	P. Black,
Bearden, Edwin B.	Meek, Mary F.	16 Apr 1850	W.T. Plummer, MG
Erwin, James G.	Pat(c?)e, Lucy Catharine	1 Jun 1850	Nero H. Grove, Sec.
Dugger, Shadrach S.	Lamere, Martha Jane	18 Jul 1850	Joseph Brown, MG
Anderson, William B.	Collins, Elizabeth	28 Aug 1850	N. Hays, JP
Shields, William F.	Moore, Martha A.	17 Sep 1850	H.K. Shields, MG
Mason, Isaac N.	Scruggs, Margaret E.	2 Oct 1850	Robert Caldwell, VDM
Spivy, James	Walker, Martha	14 Oct 1850	William Henry Sanders,
Bennett, Samuel H.	Johnson, Catharine C.	14 Oct 1850	G.D. Taylor,
Roberts, William B.	Moore, Mary Ann	27 Oct 1850	Stephen Shelton,
Reed, Robert C.	Johnston, Mary Jane	11 Nov 1850	Bodenhamer, D, JP
McMacken, Andrew J.	Estes, Josephine	14 Nov 1850	James Brownlow, MG
Reed, William W.	Pitman, Mary	17 Nov 1850	H.R. Kirby, MG
Craig, William J.	Abernathy, Virginia B.	19 Nov 1850	W.T. Plummer, MG
Creecy, Jesse	Goold, Sarah Jane	2 Dec 1850	W.T. Lee,
Blewett, Thomas G.	Martin, Laura	5 Dec 1850	G.D. Taylor,

GILES COUNTY TENNESSEE MARRIAGES

GROOM	BRIDE	DATE	OFFICIAL OR SECURITY
Swinney, Briant	Roberts, Eliza	20 Dec 1850	S.A. Parsons, JP
Cox, Angenal	Edwards, Sarah(alias Doss) Antoinett	29 Dec 1850	W.G. Hensley, DME
Hancock, Noah	McDonald, Martha	21 Jan 1851	W.T. Plummer, MG
Hickman, Samuel B.	Sands, Elvira Elizabeth	25 Jan 1851	Andrew J. Hickman, Sec.
Sumner, McHenry	Lester, Adaline K.	2 Apr 1851	J.B. Sumner, Sec.
Buchanan, Milton	Bumpass, Araminta D.	7 Apr 1851	A. D. Smith, Sec.
Ballentine, George W.	Childress, Mary G.	25 Apr 1851	C. P. Reece, MG
Jones, Isaac L.	Meadows, Mary E.	23 Apr 1851	Flemon B. McBroom, Sec.
Hays, Francis M.	Glenn, Elizabeth M.	11 Jun 1851	William S. A. Estes, Sec.
Evans, Henry	Dodson, Mary Ann	7 Jul 1851	Whitfield Dodsen, Sec.
Smith, Willis E.	Barnett, Frances I.	7 Aug 1851	James Hanna, JP
Helmick, Andrew J.	Burgess, Mary	18 Spe 1851	J. William Lee,
Phillips, William J.	Pace, Louisa Jane	18 Sep 1851	Peter Shulen, JP
Trice, Samuel	Lovell, Lina	13 Nov 1851	_____ Brownlow, JP
Smith, Franklin H.	Atkins, Mary Ann	20 Nov 1851	John Reese,
Seck, Hardin P.	Hale, Mary Elizabeth	1 Feb 1852	William Tinnan, JP
Dickerson, Augustine	Pace, Rachel	29 Feb 1852	Peter Shulen, JP
Holt, Eli	Green, Delilah	18 Mar 1852	J.V. Vandiveer, MG
Walker, Albert A.	Ballentine, Margaret J.	22 Apr 1852	W. T. Plummer, MG
Sisk, John	Swinney, Martha Jane	31 May 1852	Thos. C. McCracken, JP
Swinney, Richard H.	Dyer, Sarah A.	20 Jun 1852	Jas. C. Stevenson,
Bonds, Alfred S.	Kincaid, Mary Elizabeth	27 Jun 1852	B. W. White, MCC
Rogers, John	Haley, Caroline	8 Sep 1852	John Reese,
Holder, William	Montgomery, Mrs. Lucy	24 Sep 1852	William Perry, JP
Gilmore, John	McDaniel, Sarah	29 Sep 1852	Peter Shylen, JP
Abernathy, James E.	Denty, Susanna Rebecca	4 Oct 1852	W. T. Plummer, MG
Puckett, Lewis P.	Pitman, Nancy	4 Oct 1852	John R.S. Kendrick,(x),Sec.
Coleman, Alexander	Newton, Nancy Jane	6 Oct 1852	J.A. Beall, JP
Bramlett, Franklin M.	May, Penelope	7 Oct 1852	G.D. Taylor,
Cochran, James	Segraves, Mary A.	14 Oct 1852	Peter Shulen, JP
Rosson, Edmund B.	Neely, Ann E.	19 Oct 1852	Wm.G. Hensley, MG

GILES COUNTY TENNESSEE MARRIAGES

GROOM	BRIDE	DATE	OFFICIAL OR SECURITY
Julian, Armina T.	Mitchell, Elizabeth C.	1 Nov 1852	W.S. Adkins, Sec.
Young, Joseph	Huff, Rebecca	4 Nov 1852	James C. Stevenson,
Harwell, Wesley	McCracken, Lucinda Jane	8 Nov 1852	T.M. Harwell, MG
Morrison, Wm. A.	McCollum, Louisa	18 Nov 1852	Wm. G. Hensley, MG
Gandney, Wyatt	Evetts, Lucinda	19 Nov 1852	William Inman, JP
Petty, Robert J.	Cook, Mary E.	30 Nov 1852	N. Hays, JP
Huff, John S.W.	Cox, Amanda	30 Nov 1852	W.P.Kincaid,LEMECS
Flippen, Joseph	Morton, Olly	1 Dec 1852	Bill Booth, JP
Ross, Joab F.	Hazlewood, Nancy J.	23 Dec 1852	John P.C. Reed, JP
Brown, Wm. F.	Graves, Nancy Catharine	22 Dec 1852	M.H. Butler,
Felker, Wm. H.	Anderson, Thirza Jane	25 Dec 1852	Harrison D. Hart, JP
Abernathy, Henry M.C.	Graves, Alcy Caroline	25 Dec 1852	C.H. Lambeth, JP
Bowers, Edward D	Cardin, Mary Frances	27 Apr 1853	Jas. L. Baugh, Sec.
Bales, John M.	Clardy, Sarah Ann Jane	29 Apr 1853	Nathaniel Clardy(x),Jr,Sec
Husbands, Miles H.	Gardner, Eliza A.	29 Jun 1853	Adam S. Riggs, MG
Johnson, Matthew M.	White, Mary F.	14 Jul 1853	Alexander Smith, MG
Ezell, A.V.	Perkins, Julia A.	8 Sep 1853	William Levesque,MG
Ferguson, Daniel S.	Combs, Mary T.	15 Sep 1853	Adam S. Riggs, MG
Swinney, Jesse	Robards, Eliza	5 Oct 1853	W.T. Plummer, MG
Cryer, Elijah	Lassiter, Elizabeth	7 Nov 1853	J.W. Hargroves, Sec.
Garner, Abraham	Tankersley, Cynthia	13 Nov 1853	unreadable
Archer, James B.T.	Speer, Isabella	2 Dec 1853	Robert Caldwell,VDM
Penny, James A.J.	Sandusky, Milly	25 Jan 1855	Wm. Wood, JP.
Hagood, James J.	Waldrup, Sarah Caroline	28 Jan 1855	Thomas H. Noblitt,JP.
Alexander, Henry J.	Hopkins, Rebecca	8 Feb 1855	L.A. Parsons, JP
Wilkes, Wm. H.	Holt, Malvina A.	3 Apr 1855	Wm.D. Uleas (Wear?)MG
Carroll, Wm. E.	Morrow, Margaret M.	7 May 1855	John M. Hewitt, JP
Pettus, John W.	Waters, Sarah F.	10 Jul 1855	John E. Gilbert, Sec.
Pullen, Robert M.	Suttle, Sarophina	27 Aug 1855	G.D. Taylor,
Wright, William	Hughs, Martha Jane	30 Aug 1855	Wm. Levesque, MG
Grubbs, Sterling C.	Abernathy, Dinicia E.	20 Sep 1855	John H. Birdsong,
Tacker, Joshua L.	Wilsford, Zella R.	20 Sep 1855	Geo. T. Malone, JP
Webb, Wm. N.	Allison, Rhoda	15 Oct 1855	E.H. McCord, JP

GILES COUNTY TENNESSEE MARRIAGES

GROOM	BRIDE	DATE	OFFICIAL OR SECURITY
Teip,(?),Geo. W.	White, Elizabeth	25 Oct 1855	J.V. Vandiver, MG
Hambleton, Jacob C.	Franks, Mary Jane	9 Nov 1855	David Crook,
Locke, Pleasant C.	Newell, Batheny C.	6 Nov 1855	D.H. Jones, MG
Farmer, Joseph M.	Mitchell, Fanton O.	11 Nov 1855	Wm. Fry, JP
Daniel, Tilman M.	Meredith, Mary E.	13 Nov 1855	C.P. Reece,
Compton, Dewitt C.	Gibson, Nancy M.	6 Dec 1855	Wm. Peaton, JP.
Moore, James	Long, Sarah Jane	19 Dec 1855	Thos. H. Noblitt, JP
Petty, Daniel R.	Buchanan, Martha A.	20 Dec 1855	D.Bodenhamer, JP
Jordon, Alexander	Tucker, Mary Ann	23 Dec 1855	Martin Griggs, JP
Fogg, William	Merris, Sarah L.	18 Dec 1855	Rev.A.J. Gilmore.
Bell, John	Coleman, Ann P.	26 Dec 1855	C.H. Lambeth,
Hollis, Alexander	Haley, Eliza D.	30 Dec 1855	G.W. Bass, JP
Webb, Jacob	Lucy, Elizabeth Ann	27 Jan 1856	G.W. Bass, JP
Vaughan, Charles	Pollock, Rachel	25 Feb 1856	S.A. Parsons, JP
Martin, James	Flippen, Roda	11 Mar 1856	Bell Burch, JP
Smith, Wm.C.	Harwell, Mary Jane	21 Apr 1856	Giles M. Meek, Sec.
Hamlett, John W.	Bearden, Lucy Ann	1 May 1856	S.A. Parsons, JP
Lock, Sidney	Lock, Sarah Jane	25 May 1856	James Hanna, JP
Mitchell, Jas.O.	Angus, Mary F.	14 Aug 1856	Wm. Fry, JP
Tucker, William	Polston, Mary	17 Aug 1856	Willis M.Stevenson,JP
Wilson, Boon	Derr, Polly Ann	21 Aug 1856	J.W. Lee,
Woldridge, Andrew J.	Woldridge, Elizabeth	26 Aug 1856	H.K. Shields, MG
High, Wm. R.	Meals, Mary E.	15 Sep 1856	John Franklin, Sec.
Coleman, Jas. L.	Lester, Catharine A.	2 Oct 1856	G.D. Taylor,
Simmons, John W.	Moore, Isabell N.	4 Oct 1856	Allen E. May, Sec.
Garrett, Adison B.	Keath, Martha	24 Oct 1856	W.B. Hardy, Sec. John P.C. Reed, JP
Hester, Allen Y.	Hardy, Mary Ann	23 Oct 1856	John P.C. Reed, JP
Pamplin, Wm. L.	Osburn, Mary	5 Nov 1856	Jacob M. Bass, Sec.
Walker, George W.	Pillow, Ruth E.V.	20 Nov 1856	P.L. ___unreadable
Wisdon, Leander	Prior, Louisa Jane	25 Nov 1856	J.V. Vandiver, MG
Gant, W.J.	Webb, Rebecca J.	3 Dec 1856	John William Lee,
Snow, David	Marten, Hester Anne	3 Dec 1856	S.A. Parsons, JP
Gregory, Bird	Forbes, Purlina Jane	9 Dec 1856	John A.___, JP

GILES COUNTY TENNESSEE MARRIAGES

GROOM	BRIDE	DATE	OFFICIAL OR SECURITY
Kelso, Nicholas M.	Pack, Mary M.	20 Dec 1856	S.A. Parsons,
Hays, James T.	Puyors, Indiana C.	24 Dec 1856	N.R. Gilmore, MG
Nance, James	Ingram, Sarah	2 Apr 1857	F.M. Hills, JP
Claxton, Isaac	Self, Jane	12 Apr 1857	S.A. Parsons, JP
McNeese, Wm. R.	Howard, Emily C.	16 Apr 1857	Wm. Perry, JP
Clark, Boon	Beard, Mary Ann	31 May 1857	Hardin Griggs, JP
Grisler, Ferdinand Julius	Drumons, Eliza	4 Aug 1857	J.D. Goodrum, JP
Pillow, Stephen R.	Castleberry, Jane	20 Oct 1857	Wm. Peaton, JP
Patterson, James	Reynolds, Mary T.	4 Nov 1857	W.T. Plummer, EME
Hill, Jasper	Webb, Louisa	31 Dec 1857	Thos. H. Noblitt, JP
Baird, Wm. H.	Gordon, Mary Jane	4 Jan 1858	L.M. Harwell,
Horn, James	Barnes, Susan F.	17 Jan 1858	S.A. _____, MG
Dickey, John M.	Hale, Elizabeth C.	20 Jan 1858	J.V. Vandiveer, MG
Grant, James F.	Mays, Julia F.	2 Feb 1858	J. Sherrill, MG
Tarpley, Wm. A.	Carter, Mary Jane	28 Jan 1858	Wm. P. Woodson,
Potts, Lewis W.	Daugherty, Sarah	31 Jan 1858	John M. Kelly, JP
Arrowsmith, Wm.	Wilkerson, Mary E.	31 Jan 1858	J.C. Putman, MG
McCafety, James	Jones, Nancy	4 Feb 1858	Thos. H. Noblitt, JP
Harris, David C.	Holt, Averina	11 Feb 1858	James C. Stevenson,
Conley, John B.	Conley, Susan Virginia	16 Feb 1858	W.G. Hensley, MG
Marler, William	Griggs, Mary Ann	28 Feb 1858	S.A. Parsons, JP
Hazelwood, John P.	Hardeman, Sarah Jane	7 Mar 1858	John Hughes, JP
Greer, Joseph W.	Newman, Mary Jane	18 Mar 1858	John A._____,
Weatherford, Wm. B.	Thurman, Lucy E. Residence of Willis Thurman.	21 Mar 1858	John S. Williams, MG
Morris, John W.	Tinnon, Lucretia	25 Mar 1858	H.P. McMillian, JP
Freeman, Reubin B.	Swinebroad, Nancy D.E.	30 Mar 1858	James C. Elliott, MG
Kilburn, James H.	Norton, Lucinda	28 Mar 1858	Calloway H. Tidwell, JP
Gordon, Andrew R.	Dickerson, Rebecca	15 Apr 1858	Alexander Smith, MG
Doss, James M.	Harmon, Mary Jane	30 May 1858	J. Wm. Lee,
Thompson, Andrew J.	Barr, Nancy	18 Jun 1858	Thos. H. Noblett, JP
Walls, John	Ward, Palina	14 Jul 1858	Stephen Odenell, JP
Alley, William	Norton, Amanda	15 Jul 1858	Wm. Peaton, JP
Lucy, Henry W.	Joins, Amanda A.	19 Aug 1858	John S. Wilks, MG

GROOM	BRIDE	DATE	OFFICIAL OR SECURITY
Comer, Robert	McMasters, Sarah E.	7 Sep 1858	Thos. H. Noblett, JP
Trice, James P.	Lovell, Louisa	29 Sep 1858	Jesse Fry, JP
Connor, Wm. E.	Carter, Mary E.	5 Oct 1858	E. Hanks, MG
Moore, Robert W.	Watkins, Nancy Jane	7 Oct 1858	H.P. Stanley, JP
Strong, Edmund	Norman, Permelia E.	4 Nov 1858	C.H. Lambeth, JP
Scott, Wm. H.	Eason, Mariah L.	10 Nov 1858	John H. Birdsong,
McNairy, John F.	Black, Martha Ann	16 Nov 1858	Robert Caldwell,VDM
Montgomery, Alexander	Hayes, Eliza M.	7 Dec 1858	J. William Lee,
Ezell, Marion P.	Tarplay, Mary E.	16 Dec 1858	Jas. C. Stevenson,
Ramsey, Wm.	Hale, Sarah Jane	16 Dec 1858	A.H. Berry,
Young, Joseph	McKnight, Lucy	23 Dec 1858	L.D. Harwell, MG
English, John T.	Lock, Sarah B.	6 Jan 1859	William Peaton, JP
Hamersley, Robert A.	Alsup, Mary F.	7 Jan 1859	Jas. A. Warren, JP
Witt, Carter H.	Bugg, Sarah E.	8 Jan 1859	Jesse Fry, JP
Malone, Robert M.	Shields, Camilla A.	9 Jan 1859	H.K. Shields, MG
Nave, Alexander H.	Cobb, Susannah	10 Jan 1859	unsigned
Hicks, Joseph N.	Miller, Louisa Z.	12 Jan 1859	J.C. Inman, JP
Lanier, Edmund	Cooper, Mary	12 Jan 1859	_____Rose, JP
Rambo, Marcus	Duke, Martha	13 Jan 1859	John M. Kelley, JP
Quals, John R.	Emerson, Elizabeth C.	13 Jan 1859	James Brownlow, MG
Jones, Wm. R.	Hannah, Margaret M.	20 Jan 1859	Jos. L. Edmundson, JP
Spencer, Isaac N.	Williams, Martha	27 Jan 1859	James Brownlow, MG
Waldrup, William	Bearden, Frances	30 Jan 1859	Jesse Fry, JP
Erwin, Leonidas	Bonds, Zipporah	1 Feb 1859	Hardin Griggs, JP
Foster, William	Ward, Malena Ann	10 Feb 1859	Stephen Od____,JP
Cox, Samuel	Jackson, Polly Ann	3 Feb 1859	James A. Warren,JP
Ayres, James E.	Crutcher, Sarah A.	6 Feb 1859	B.M. Gallary,
Featherston, John	Knight, Eliza J.	17 Feb 1859	John M. Hewitt, JP
Allen, John M.	Sparkman, Emanthe P.	20 Feb 1859	J.P. Richardson,MG
Lanier, Wm. S.	Cobbs, Sarah Ann	20 Feb 1859	Gilbert W. Bass, JP
Wilks, Leroy W.	Doggett, Narcissa B.	24 Feb 1859	B. McCollum,
Treedy, Lewis	Covington, Lucinda	27 Feb 1859	James A. Warren,JP
Parker, John A.	Baker, Eliza G.	1 Mar 1859	John S. Williams,MG
Cox, Dr. Geo. W.	Moore, Amanda C.	1 Mar 1859	W.L. Tarbut, DVM

GILES COUNTY TENNESSEE MARRIAGES

GROOM	BRIDE	DATE	OFFICIAL OR SECURITY
Scoggin, Robert M.	Mosby, Lucy K.	8 Mar 1859	R. Caldwell, VDM
McQuigg, Henry K.	Evans, Sarah L.	10 Mar 1859	Jesse Fry, JP
Rogers, Thomas	Sutton, Sarah M.	15 Mar 1859	B. McCollum, JP
Madry, John P.	Etenton, Julia A.F.	15 Mar 1859	A.M. Kerr,
Smith, Edward	Hastin, Sarah E.	27 Mar 1859	John M. Kelly, JP
Kettner, Robert F.	McCaslin, Amanda A.	31 Mar 1859	John M. Hewitt, JP
Poteet, James S.	Magee, M.K.	15 Apr 1859	William Peaton, JP
Griffin, Wm.	Hogan, Mary	20 Apr 1859	A.W. Walker, MG
Nance, Wm.	McMurry, Margaret D.	26 Apr 1859	H.K. Shields, MG
Westmoreland, Jerome W.	Deaver, Mary Ann	2 May 1859	J.W. Whitten, MG
Bennet, Thomas	Toole, Bridget	10 May 1859	John Scollard,
Moore, Wm. T.	Gilmore, Sarah J.	9 Jun 1859	J.H. Strayhorn, MG
Hester, John W.	Smith, Rebecca E.	12 Jun 1859	Jas. A. Warren, JP
McKimmin, Andrew J.	Everly, George Anna	7 Jun 1859	Robert Caldwell, VDM
Davis, Jarome	Marlow, Winey M.	21 Jul 1859	S.A. Parsons, JP
Todd, Archibald A.	Simms, Manervy C.	18 Sep 1859	Andrew Smith, MG
Hindman, Elihu	Bailey, Sarah E.	8 Oct 1859	W.M. Hawkins, JP
Bell, Uriah	Warren, Elmina M.	16 Nov 1859	McHenry Sumner, MG
Phelps, Thos. B.	Loyd, Simantha E.	17 Nov 1859	L.D. Harwell,
Cross, Wm.	Smith, Sarah	29 Nov 1859	H.K. Shields, MG
Brownlow, John P.	Ussery, Hester J.	1 Dec 1859	William Peaton, JP
Dunavant, Joseph H.	Stuart, Susannah	2 Dec 1859	Wm. Peaton, JP
Knight, Wm. R.	Baugh, Rosannah	8 Dec 1859	Jos. E. White, MME
Ingram, Jonas M.	Waldrup, Nancy J.	9 Dec 1859	W.M. Hawkins, JP
Rogers, Stephen H.	James, Elviry J.	8 Dec 1859	B.M. Galloway, MG
Strong, Thomas	Lun, Elizabeth	26 Dec 1859	B.W. Knight, JP
White, Elijah	Johnson, Sally	2 Jan 1860	A.M. Kerr,
Parker, Alfred W.	Flaught, Mary C.	15 Jan 1860	Z. Parker, MG
Madegan, Dennis	Manly, Margarett Arlena	22 Jan 1860	N. Hays, JP
Bodenhamer, John L.	Howard, Harriett A.	23 Jan 1860	Jas. R. Horner, Sec.
Carter, Jas. M.	Lock, Eliza M.	29 Jan 1860	W.N. Watkins, JP
Rea, John T.	Parker, Mildren E.	2 Feb 1860	Wm. Peaton, JP
Mitchell, Henry T.	Kimbrough, Nancy B.	3 Feb 1860	W.T. Appleton, Sec.

GILES COUNTY TENNESSEE MARRIAGES

GROOM	BRIDE	DATE	OFFICIAL OR SECURITY
Abernathy, Isaah	Birdsong, Mary Ann	26 Feb 1860	Gilbert W. Bass, JP
Murrell, Calvin C.	Randolph Martha	15 Mar 1860	R.F. Buchanan, JP
Causby, Lewis	Galloway, Sarah	22 Mar 1860	A.H. Berry,
Tennison, John S.	Kelly, Malinda Jane	8 Apr 1860	Jas. A. Warren, JP
Cobb, Willis M.	Dean, Louisa C.	27 Jun 1860	Jas. A. Warren, JP
McMillian, James L.	Moore, Sarah M.	12 Jul 1860	C.W. McMillian, JP
Williams, Geo. W.	Rochel, Elizabeth	26 Jul 1860	John S. Butler, JP
Hamonsly, John B.	Hunter, Sarah A.	31 Jul 1860	Thomas Hanna, JP
Bell, Jonathan C.	Barmore, Mary	13 Aug 1860	Robt. Caldwell, VDM
Flaught, Madison	Coats, Sarah Ann	30 Aug 1860	John A. Coats, Sec.
Stovall, Thomas M.	Stephenson, Sarah E.	6 Sep 1860	Jas. C. Stevenson,
Garrett, Isham S.	Brownlow, Elizabeth C.	22 Sep 1860	John L. Butler, JP
Cochran, James B.	Williamson, Martha R.	7 Oct 1860	H.K. Shields, MG
Carter, Thomas T.	Haynes, Mary E.	11 Oct 1860	D.V. Vandiveer, MG
Hill, Wm.D.S.	Newman, Tempy L.	23 Oct 1860	E.B. Stamps, JP
Bradley, Moten	Tucker, Martha Ann	3 Nov 1860	H.P. Stanley, JP
Menetree, David G.	Clark, Manerva	20 Nov 1860	Jas. C. Stevenson,
Caruthers, Woodson	Abernathy, Louisa	21 Nov 1860	C.W. McMillian, JP
Bray, John B.	Hogan, Rebecca	29 Nov 1860	W.T. Ussery,
Nip,(Niss?), Daniel	Dunavant, Mary R.	3 Dec 1860	Wm. F. Simpson, JP
Horn, James R.	Wagstaff, Virginia A.	20 Dec 1860	David H. Parsons, JP
Wood, John M.	Bentley, Helen M.	20 Dec 1860	H.K. Shields, MG
Burge, John F.	Causby, Frances	20 Dec 1860	Thos. S. Pittard, Sec.
Murry, James M.	Williams, Mary E.	24 Dec 1860	Josiah Boyett, Sec.
Dunnivant, A.A.	Garrett, Abegale	24 Dec 1860	P.H. Dunnivant, Sec.
Gatlin, James T.	Browning, Sarah M.	24 Dec 1860	S.P. Rhea, Sec.
Kercy, William	Blow, Sarah A.	25 Jan 1861	J.W. Lee, MG
McLaurine, Wm. P.	Loyd, Mary Frances	7 Feb 1861	L.D. Harwell,
Shors, Wm. M.	Judkins, Martha A.	10 Feb 1861	Wm. Gilmore,
Duger, Thomas M.	Glenn, Martha	15 Feb 1861	James Kirkland, MG
Kirkpatrick, Wm. H.	Ezell, Mattie M.	14 Feb 1861	L.D. Harwell,
Hendrix, John B.	Hogan, Cornelia C.	3 Mar 1861	A.W. Walker, MG
Warren, Wm. W.	Bee, Mary E.	21 Mar 1861	D.H. Jones, MG

GILES COUNTY TENNESSEE MARRIAGES

GROOM	BRIDE	DATE	OFFICIAL OR SECURITY
Hickman, Willis H.	Thurman, Sarah E.	7 April 1861	John S. Williams,
Watson, Samuel H.	Massy, Rebecca Ann	28 Apr 1861	Hardin Griggs, JP
Mo-----, Silas	Smith, Sarah Jane	30 Apr 1861	James Shelton, Pr G.
Samuels, Wm. S.	Carmical, Rebecca C.	2 Jun 1861	L.D. Harwell,
Armstrong, Jas. J.	Thornton, Elizabeth F.	5 Sep 1861	H.P. Stanley, JP
Hogin, Anderson	Hale, Asenath	15 Oct 1861	James Shelton, Pr.G.
Rhea, Thomas H.	Brown, Sarah E.	10 Nov 1861	Thos. H. Noblitt, JP
Inman, Luke T.	Reagin, Samierancey?	19 Nov 1861	Jos. S. Edmondson, JP
Bullock, Howel C.	Reynolds, Josephine	11 Dec 1861	G.D. Taylor,
Madison, Wm. J.	Abernathy, Mindosa B.	12 Mar 1862	John G. Abernathy, JP
Gilliam, Isaac	Thurman, Letsy	22 Mar 1862	David Angus, JP
Page, George W.	Bratton, Louisa	13 Apr 1862	David H. Parsons, JP
Freeman, Daniel M.	Abernathy, Elizabeth	15 Apr 1862	R.G. Kimbrough, MG
Garner, William H.	Rockley, Louisa E.	26 Apr 1862	Jesse S. Jones, Sec.
Shook, George	Elwin?, Mary	29 Jun 1862	David H. Parsons, JP
Harrison, James	George, Sarah	13 Jul 1862	no return
Clinton, Samuel	Rogers, Mary Ann	13 Aug 1862	Jas. C. Stevenson,
Woodard, Hiram C.	Barnfield, Martha	3 Sep 1862	James C. Stevenson,
McKnight, Frank L.	Young, Mary E.	9 Oct 1862	L.D. Harwell,
Jordan, John	Duncan, Sarah M.	9 Oct 1862	Robert Caldwell, VDM
Moses, Henry C.	Johnson, Elizabeth Ann	15 Oct 1862	Wm. Gilman,
Williams, Willoughby	Belew, Jane	30 Oct 1862	C.P. Reed,
Gatlin, John	King, Sarah	29 Oct 1862	S.P. Rhea, Sec.
Herman, Stephen D.	Redus, Celestia C.	26 Nov 1862	B. Fuller, MG
Bates, John B.	Jordan, Aramanda S.	25 Nov 1862	Wm. Tinsley, Sec.
Newsoms, Lewis	McGreer, Catharine	24 Dec 1862	L.D. Harwell,

Abernathy, Adaline 1
" Dinicia E. 5
" Elizabeth 11
" Henry M.C. 5
" Isaah 10
" James E. 4
" John G. 11
" Louisa 10
" Mindosa B. 11
" Richard 1
" Virginia B. 3
Adkins, W.S. r
Alexander, Henry J. 5
Allen, John M. 8
Alley, Wm. 7
Allison, Rhoda 5
Alsup, Mary F. 8
Anderson, Thirza Jane 5
" William B. 3
Angus, David 11
" Mary F. 6
" Mary T. 2
Apperson, Lucy S. 1
Appleton, W. T. 9
Archer, James B.T. 5
Armstrong, James J. 11
Arrowsmith, William 7
Arthur, Henry D. 2
Atkins, Mary Ann 4
Ayres, James E. 8

Baily, Sarah E. 9
Baird, William H. 7
Baker, Eliza B. 8
Bales, John M. 5
Ballentine, Geo. W. 4
" Margaret J. 4
Barmore, Mary 10
Barnes, George W. 2
" Susan F. 7
" Uriah E. 2
Barnett, Frances I. 4
Barnfield, Martha 11
Barr, Nancy, 2,7
Bates, John B. 11
Baugh, Jas. L. 5
" Rosannah 9
Bass, Gilbert W. 6,8,10
Beale, Lilly 1
" J.A. 4
Beard, Mary Ann 7
Bearden, Edwin B. 3
" Frances 8
" Lucy Ann 6

Beaver, Lemuel 1
Beckham, Wm. J. 3
Bee, Mary E. 10
Belew, Jane 11
Bell, John 6
" Jonathan C. 10
Bell, Uriah 9
Bennett, Samuel H. 3
Bennett, Thomas 9
Bentley, Helen M. 10
Berry, A. H. 8,10
Birdsong, Jeff 3
" John H. 3,5,8
" Mary Ann 10
Black, Martha Ann 8
" P. 3
Blewett, Thomas G. 3
Blow, Sarah A. 10
Bodenhamer, D. 3,6
Bodenhamer, John L. 9
Bonds, Alfred S. 4
" Zipporah 8
Booth, Bill 5
" Therra 3
Bowers, Edward D. 5
Boyett, Josiah 10
Bradley, Mary Ann 1
" Moten 10
Bramlett, Franklin M. 4
Bratton, Louisa 11
Bray, John B. 10
Briggs, Frances S. 3
" Maria A. 1
Brooks, Joanna 1
Brookshire, Josiah 2
" Minerva G. 2
Browning, Sarah M. 10
Brownlow, ____ 4
" Elizabeth 1
" Elizabeth C. 10
" James 3,8
" John P. 9
Brown, Beverly 1
" H.H. 1(2)
" Ira E. 1,2(2)
" Irvin R. 1
" Joseph 3
" Mary E. 3
" Sarah E. 11
" Wm. F. 5
" Wm. R. 1
Bryan, John W. 1
Buchanan, Martha A. 6
" Milton 4

INDEX TO GILES COUNTY TENNESSEE MARRIAGES

Buchanan, R. F. 10
Buford, Nicholas C. 2
Bugg, Sarah E. 8
Bullock, Howel C. 11
Bumpass, Araminta D. 4
Burch, Mary C. 1
Burge, John F. 10
Burgess, John 3
    " Mary 4
Burnett, Thomas M. 2
Burrow, Nancy H. 1
Busick, J.M. 1
Butcher, Joshua 1
Butler, John (L or S)10(2)
    " M.H. 5

Caldwell, Robert 2,3,5,8,
  9(2),11
Calhoun, Warren W. 2
Cardin, Mary Frances 5
Carmical, Rebecca C. 11
Carrell, James 3
Carroll, William E. 5
Carter, Eliza Jane 3
    " James M. 9
    " Mary E. 8
    " Mary Jane 7
    " Nancy 2
    " Thomas T. 10
Caruthers, Woodson 10
Castleberry, Franklin 1
    " Jane 7
Causby, Frances 10
    " Lewis 10
Childress, Mary G. 4
Clanton, Wm. T. 2
Clardy, Nathaniel 5
    " Sarah Ann Jane 5
Clark, Boon 7
  C Manerva 10
    " William M. 2
Claxton, Isaac 7
Clinton, Samuel 11
Coats, John A. 10
    " Sarah Ann 10
Cobb(s), Sarah Ann 8
    " Susannah 8
    " Willis M. 10
Cochran, James 4
    " James B. 10
Coleman, Alexander 4
    " Ann P. 6
    " Jas. L. 6
Collins, Elizabeth 3
    " Maria 2

Combs, Mary T. 5
Comer, Robert 8
Compton, Dewitt C. 6
Conley, John B. 7
    " Susan Virginia 7
Connor, William E. 8
Conoly, Archibald 1
Cook, Mary E. 5
Cooper, Mary 8
Covington, Lucinda 8
Cox, Amanda 5
    " Angenal 4
    " Dr. Geo. W. 8
    " Samuel 8
Craig, William B. 2
    " William J. 3
Creecy, Jesse 3
Crook, David 1,6
Cross, William 9
Crutcher, Sarah A. 8
Cryer, Elijah 5
Curry, Alfred 2
Curtis, Isaiah 2
    " James W. 2

Daggett, Miller 3
Daniel, Tilman M. 6
Daugherty, Sarah 7
Davenport, Matthew 1
Davidson, Butler 1
    " George W. 1
Davis, Jerome 9
    " William 1
Dean, Louisa C. 10
Deaver, Mary Ann 9
Deaty, Susannah Rebecca 4
Derr, Polly Ann 6
Devasier, Minerva Caroline 3
Dickerson, Augustine 4
    " Cynthia B. 2
    " Rebecca 7
Dickey, John M. 7
    " Margaret 1
Dodso(e)n, John M. 3
    " Lydia Jane 1
    " Mary Ann 1
    " Whitfield 4
Doggett, Narcissa B. 8
Doss, James M. 7
    " Sarah Antoinett 4
Doyle, Nance 2
Drumons, Eliza 7
Dugger, Shadrach S. 3
Duger, Thomas M. 10
Duke, Martha 8

14

Dunavant, Joseph H. 9
"   Mary R. 10
Duncan, Sarah M. 11
Dunn, William D. 2
Dunnivant, A.A. 10
"   P.H. 10
Dyer, Sarah A. 4

Eason, Mariah L. 8
Edmondson, Jos. S. 11
Edwards, John 1
"   Nancy 1
"   Sarah Antoinett 4
Elliott, James C. 7
Elwin, Mary 11
Emerson, Elizabeth C. 8
English, John T. 8
Erwin, James G. 1,2,3
"   Leonidas 8
"   Robert W. 2
Estes, Josephine 3
"   William S.A. 4
Etenton, Julia A.P. 9
Evans, Henry 4
"   Sarah L. 9
Everly, George Anna 9
Evetts, Lucinda 5
Ezell, A.V. R
"   Caroline F. 2
"   Marion P. 8
"   Mattie M. 10
"   P.H. 1

Farmer, Joseph M. 6
"   Nancy A. 2
"   Sam S. 2
Featherston, John 8
Felkner, Wm. H. 5
Ferguson, Daniel S. 5
Flaught, Madison 10
"   Mary C. 9
Flippen, Joseph 5
"   Rhoda 6
Fogg, Wm. 6
Follis, Wm. R. 3
Forbes, Purlina Jane 6
Foster, Wm. 8
Foust, Samuel R. 3
France, Martha 1
Franklin, John 6
Franks, Mary Jane 6
Frazier, Julia 2
Freeman, Daniel M. 11
"   Joel E. 2
"   Reubin B. 7

Fry, Jesse 8(3),9
"   William 6(2)
Fuller, B. 11
"   Caid 3
"   John 3

Gaines, James 1
Gallary, B. M. 8
Galloway, B.H. 9
"   Sarah 10
Gant, W.J. 6
Gandney, Wyatt 5
Gardner, Eliza A. 5
"   George W. 2
"   Jane 3
Garner, Abraham 5
"   William H. 11
Garrett, Abigale 10
"   Adison B. 6
"   Elizabeth B. 2
"   Isham S. 10
"   Sarah 3
Gatlin, James T. 10
"   John 11
George, Sarah 11
Gibson, George M. 1
Gibson, Nancy M. 6
Gilbert, John E. 5
Gilliam, Isaac 11
Gilman, William 11
Gilmore, Rev. A.J. 6
Gilmore, John 4
Gilmore, N. R. 7
"   Sarah J. 9
"   William 10
Gladish, Joshua B. 1
Glenn, Elizabeth M. 4
"   Martha 10
Goodrum, J.D. 7
Goold, Sarah Jane 3
Gordon, Andrew R. 7
"   Elizabeth 2
"   Mary Jane 7
Graham, Alexander 2
"   James P. 1
Grant, James F. 7
Graves, Alcy Caroline 5
"   Nancy Catharine 5
Green, Delilah 4
"   Robert 2
Greer, Joseph W. 7
Gregory, Bird 6
Griffin, William 9
Griggs, Hardin 7,8,11
Griggs, Martin 6

15

Griggs, Mary Ann 7
Grisler, Ferdinand Julius 7
Grove, Nero H. 3
Grubbs, Sterling C. 5

Hackney, Eveline Tennessee 1
Hagood, James J. 5
Hale, Asenath 11
" Elizabeth C. 7
" Mary Elizabeth 4
" Sarah Jane 8
Haley, Caroline 4
" Eliza D. 6
Hambleton, Jacob C. 6
Hamersley, Robert A. 8
Hamlett, John W. 6
Hammons, Matilda 1
Hamonsly, John B. 10
Hancock, Noah 4
Hanks, E. 8
Hanna, James 4,6
" Martha A. 2
" Thomas 10
Hannah, Margaret M. 8
Hardeman, Sarah Jane 7
Hardy, Mary Ann 6
Hardy, W. B. 6
Hargrove, J. W. 5
" William A. 1
Harmond, Mary Jane 7
Harris, David C. 7
Harrison, James 1,11
Harrison, Mary Ann 1
Hart, Harrison D. 5
Harwell, Ladoca Ann 2
" L.D. 8,9,10(2),11(3)
" L.M. 7
" Mary Jane 6
" T.M. 3,5
" Wesley 5
Hastin, Sarah E. 9
Hawkins, W. M. 9(2)
Hay(e)s, Eliza M. 8
" Francis M. 4
" James T. 7
" N. 3,5,9
Haynes, Mary E. 10
Hazelwood, John P. 7
" Nancy J. 5
Helmick, Andrew J. 4
Hendrix, John B. 10
Hensley, W. G. 4(3),5,7
Herman, Stephen D. 11
Hester, Allen Y. 6
" John W. 9

Hewitt, John M. 5,8,9
Hickman, Andrew J. 4
" Samuel B. 4
" Willis H. 11
Hicks, Joseph N. 8
High, William R. 6
Hill(s), Allen 1
" F. M. 7
" Jasper 7
" Milton 1
" William D.S. 10
Hillhouse, Mary Caroline 2
Hindman, Elihu 9
Hogan, Anderson 1,11
" Cornelia C. 10
" Mary 9
" Rebecca 10
Holder, William 4
Hollis, Alexander 6
Holt, Averina 7
" Eli 4
" Malvina A. 5
Hood, Sterling C. 3
Hopkins, Rebecca 5
Hopkins, Sarah B. 1
Horn, James 7
" James R. 10
Horner, Jas. R. 9
Howard, Emily C. 7
" Harriett A. 9
" Nehemiah 2
Huff, John S.W. 5
" Rebecca 5
" Wiley 1
Hughes, John 2,7
" Martha Jane 5
Hunter, Sarah A. 10
Husbands, Miles H. 5

Ingram, Isaac 1
" Jonas M. 9
" Sarah 7
Inman, J.C. 8
" Luke T. 11
" William 2,5

Jackson, Hezekiah 2
" John B. 2
" Polly Ann 8
James, Elviry J. 9
Johnson, Catharine C. 3
" Elizabeth Ann 11
" Matthew M. 5
" Sally 9

16

INDEX TO GILES COUNTY TENNESSEE MARRIAGES

Johnston, James T. 3
"   Mary Jane 3
"   Susannah Jane 3
Joins, Amanda A. 7
Jones, D.H. 6,10
"   E.D. 1
"   Henry 1
"   Homer R. 2
"   Isaac L. 4
"   Jacob 1(3)
"   John L. 2
"   Martin S. 1
"   Nancy 7
"   Wm. R. 8
Jordon, Alexander 6
"   Amanda S. 11
"   John 11
Judkins, Martha A. 10
Julian, Armina T. 5

Keath, Martha 6
Kelly, John M. 7,8,9
Kelly, Malinda Jane 10
Kelso, Nicholas M. 7
Kendrick, John R.S. 4
Kennedy, Major A. 2
Kercy, William 10
Kerr, A.M. 9(3)
Kettner, Robert F. 9
Kilburn, James H. 7
Kimbrough, Mary E. 3
Kimbrough, Nancy B. 9
"   Romulus S. 3
Kincaid, Mary Elizabeth 4
"   William C. 3
"   W.P. 5
King, Griffin L. 1
"   Sarah 11
Kirby, H. R. 3
Kirkland, James 10
Kirkpatrick, William H. 10
Knight, B. W. 9
"   Eliza J. 8
"   William R. 9

Laird, Samuel R. 1
Lambeth, C.H. 5,6,8
Lanere, Martha Jane 3
Lanier, Edmund 8
"   William S. 8
Lassiter, Elizabeth 5
Lee, John Wm. 3,4,6(2),7,8,10
" William T. 3
Lester, Adaline K. 4
"   Catharine A. 6
"   Minerva T. 1

Levesque, Wm. 2,3,5(2)
Litterall, Jerusia Ann 2
Lock(e), Eliza M. 9
"   Pleasant C. 6
"   Sarah B. 8
"   Sarah Jane 6
"   Sidney 6
Long, Sarah Jane 6
Lovell, Lina 4
"   Louisa 8
Loyd, Mary Frances 10
"   Simantha E. 9
Lucy, Elizabeth Ann 6
"   Ferdinand P. 3
"   Henry W. 7
Luker, Ella Jane 2
"   Jesse 2
Lun, Elizabeth 9
Luna, M.V. 2
Lunbach, Sally 1

McBroom, Flemon B. 4
McCafety, James 7
McCallum-McCollum,
"   B. 8,9
"   Louisa 5
"   Sarah 1
Xantippe L. 3
McCaslin, Amanda A. 9
McCord, E.H. 5
McCormack, Reuben M. 3
McCracken, Lucinda Jane 5
"   Thomas C. 4
McDaniel, Sarah 4
McDonald, Martha 4
McEwen, John 3
McGreer, Catharine 11
McKimmin, Andrew J. 9
McKnight, Frank L. 11
"   Lucy 8
McLaurine F.T. 2
"   William P. 10
McMacken, Andrew J. 3
McMasters, Sarah E. 8
McMillian, C. W. 10(2)
"   E. 1
"   H.P. 7
"   James L. 10
"   Maria 1
McMullen, Eliza Ellen 3
McMurry, Margaret D. 9
McNairy, John F. 8
McNeese, William R. 7
McQuigg, Henry K. 9

Maddry, Buckner 1

Madegan, Dennis 9
Madison, William J. 11
Madry, John P. 9
Magee, M.K. 9
Malone, George T. 5
  "   Robert M. 8
Manly, Margarett Arlena 9
Manuel, Phillip 2
Marler, William 7
Marlow, Winey M. 9
Marten, Hester Anne 6
Martin, James 6
  "   Laura 3
Mason, Isaac 1
  "   Isaac N. 3
Masswy, E. Patrick 3
  "   Rebecca Ann 11
May(s), Allen E. 6
  "   Julia F. 7
  "   Penelope 4
Meadows, Mary E. 4
Meals, Mary E. 6
Meek, Mary F. 3
Melton, Henry 1
Menetree, David G. 10
Meredith, Mary E. 6
Miller, Henry 2
  "   Louisa Z. 8
Mitchell, Elizabeth C. 5
  "   Fanton O. 6
  "   Henry T. 9
  "   Jas. O. 6
Mo_____, Silas 11
Montgomery, Andrew 8
  "   Lucy 4
Moore, Amanda C. 8
  "   Belinda 1
  "   Cynthia Jane 3
  "   David I. 1
  "   Isabell N. 6
  "   James 1,6
  "   Joseph B. 1
  "   Martha A. 3
  "   Mary Ann 3
  "   Robert W. 8
  "   Sarah M. 10
  "   W.C. 3
  "   William T. 9
Morris, John W. 7
  "   Sarah L. 6
Morrison, William A. 4
Morrow, Margaret M. 5
Morton, Olly 5
Mosby, Lucy K. 9
Moses, Henry C. 11

Murrell, Calvin C. 10
Murrell, William 2
Murry, James M. 10
Myres, Eliza 3

Nance, James 7
  "   William 9
Nave, Alexander H. 8
  "   Jacob 2
  "   Jehu 2(2)
Neal, Ann Henry 2
  "   Robert 1
Neely, Ann E. 4
Newell, Batheny C. 6
Newsome, Lewis 11
Newton, Nancy Jane 4
Newman, Mary Jane 7
  "   Tempy L. 10
Nicholas, Thomas 2
Nip, Daniel 10
Noblitt, Thomas H. 5,6,7(3),8,11
Norman, Permelia E. 8
Norton, Amanoa 7
Norton, Lucinda 7

Od____, Stephen 8
Odenell, Stephen 7
Ogilby, Edward H. 1
Oliver, William H. 2
Orr, Thomas W. 2
Osburn, Mary 6
Owens, Lee H. 1

Pace, Louisa Jane 4
  "   Rachel 4
Pack, Mary M. 7
Page, Geo. W. 11
Pamplin, Wm. L. 6
Parker, Alfred W. 9
  "   John A. 8
  "   Mildred E. 9
  "   Z. 9
Parsons, David H. 10,11(2)
  "   S.A. 4,5,6(3),7(3),9
Pate(Pace?), Lucy Catharine 3
Patrick, Jane M. 2
Patterson, James 7
  "   Simpson A. 1
Peaton, Wm. 6,7(3),8,9(7)
Penny, James A.J. 5
Perkins, Julia A. 5
Perry, Wm. 2,7
Peterson, Thomas W. 3
Pettus, John W. 5
Petty, Daniel R. 6

Petty, Robert J. 5
Phelps, Geo. F. 1
Phelps, Thomas B. 9
Philips, Lucy Ann 1
Phillips, Wm. J. 4
Pickens, A.M. 2,3
Pillow, Ruth E.V. 6
Pillow, Stephen R. 7
Pitman, Mary 3
Pitman, Nancy 4
Pittard, Thomas S. 10
Plummer, W.T. 3(2),4(5),5,7
Pollock, Rachel 6
Polston, Mary 6
Poteet, James S. 9
Potts, Geo. H. 2
Potts, Lewis W. 7
Powers, Nancy M. 3
Powers, Robert B. 3
Price, Mary S.A. 1
Prior, Louisa Jane 6
Puckett, Lewis P. 4
Pullen, Robert M. 5
Putman, J.C. 7
Puyors, Indiana C. 7

Quals, John R. 8

Rainey, Mahala A. 3
Rambo, Marcus 8
Ramsay, Olivia Ann 2
   "   William 8
Randolph, Martha 10
Reagin, Samerancey? 11
Redus, Celestia C. 11
Reece, C.P. 4,6
Reed, C.P. 11
   "   John P.C. 5,6(2)
   "   Robert C. 3
   "   William W. 3
Reese, John 4(2)
Reid, James B. 3
Reynolds, Josephine 11
   "   Mary T. 7
Rhea, Hannah 1
   "   John T. 9
   "   S.P. 10,11
   "   Thomas H. 11
Richardson, J.P. 8
Riggs, Adam S. 5(2)
Robards, Eliza 5
Roberts, Eliza 4
   "   Wm. B. 3
Robertson, Bethana 2

Rachel, Elizabeth 10
Rockley, Louisa E. 11
Rogers, John 4
   "   Mary Ann 11
   "   Stephen H. 9
   "   Thomas 9
Rose, ____ 8
Ross, Joab F. 5
Rosson, Edmund B. 4

Samuels, William S. 11
Sanders, William Henry 3
Sands, Elvira Elizabeth 4
Sandusky, Milly 5
Scoggin, Robert M. 9
Scollard, John 9
Scott, Wm. H. 8
Scruggs, Margaret E. 3
Seamour, Martha Catharine 1
Segraves, Mary A. 4
Self, Jane 7
Shadden, Amanda M. 1
   "   Elisha M. 2
Shelton, James 11(2)
Shelton, Stephen 3
Sherrill, J. 7
Sherwood, Anna 1
Shields, Camilla A. 8
   "   H.K. 3,6,8,9(2),10(2)
   "   Wm. F. 3
Shockley, Benjamin 1
Shook, Geo. 11
Shores, James C. 2
Shors, Wm. M. 10
Shrader, Daniel G. 2
Shulen, Peter 4(2)
Shylen, Peter 4
Simmons, John W. 6
Simms, Manervy C. 9
   "   Robert H. 2
Simpson, Wm. F. 10
Sisk, John 4
Smith, Abigail 1
   "   A.D. 4
   "   Alexander 5,7
   "   Almus H. 3
   "   Andrew 9
   "   Edward 9
   "   Franklin H. 4
   "   Henry W. 2
   "   Rebecca E. 9
   "   Sarah 2,9
   "   Sarah Jane 11
   "   William C. 6

Smith, Willis E. 4
Snow, David 6
Sock, Hardin P. 4
Sparkman, Emanthe P. 8
Speer, Isabella 5
Spencer, Isaac N. 8
Spivy, James 3
Stamps, E. B. 10
"   Joseph B. 3
Stanley, H. P. 8,10,11
Stephenson, Sarah E. 10
Stevenson, James C. 4,5,7,8,
    10(2),11(2)
"   Willis M. 6
Stewart, William 3
Stone, Jane 2
Stovall, Thomas M. 10
Stratton, Mary C. 3
Strayhorn, J.H. 9
Strong, Edmund 8
"   James H. 2
"   Thomas 9
Stuart, Susannah 9
Sumner, J. P. 4
"   McHenry 4,9
Suttle, Sarophina 5
Sutton, Sarah M. 9
Swinebroad, Nancy D.E. 7
Swinney, Briant 4
"   Jesse 5
"   Martha Jane 4
"   Richard H. 4
"   William 1

Tacker, Elizabeth 2
"   Joshua L. 5
Tankersley, Cynthia 5
Tarbut, W.L. 8
Tarplay, Mary E. 8
"   Susannah 3
"   Wm. A. 7
Taylor, G.D. 1,2,3(2),
    4,5,6,11
"   James 1
"   James H. 1
"   Mary 1
Teip, Geo. W. 6
Tennison, John S. 10
Thompson, Andrew J. 7
Thornton, Elizabeth F. 11
Thurman, Letsy 11
"   Lucy E. 7
"   Sarah E. 11
"   Willis 7
Tidwell, Calloway H. 7
"   Elias 1

Tillery, Chas. M. 1
Tinnon, Lucretia 7
"   Wm. 4
Tinsley, Wm. 11
Todd, Archibald A. 9
"   Presley N. 1
Treedy, Lewis 8
Toole, Bridget 9
Trice, James P. 8
"   Samuel 4
Tucker, Martha Ann 10
"   Mary Ann 6
"   Violet 2
"   Wm. 6

Uleas, Wm. D. 5
Ussery, Hester J. 9
"   W.T. 10

Vandiver, D.V. 10
"   J.V. 4,6(3),7
Vansant, G. 1
Vassar, Martha 1
Vaughn, Charles 6
"   David 2
Vinson, Sarah Jane 3
W
Wagstaff, Virginia A. 10
Waldrup, Nancy J. 9
"   Sarah Caroline 5
"   Wm. 8
Walker, Albert A. 4
"   A.W. 9,10
"   Geo. W. 6
"   Martha 3
"   Mary A. 2
Waller, Joseph C. 3
Walls, John 7
Ward, Malina Ann 8
Ward, Palina 7
Warren, Elmina M. 9
"   H.B. 2
"   Jas. A. 8(3),9,10(2)
"   Wm. W. 10
Waters, Sarah F. 5
Watkins, Nancy Jane 8
W   W.N. 9
Watson, Samuel H. 11
Wear, Wm. D. 5
Weatherford, Wm B. 7
Webb, Jacob 6
"   Louisa 7
"   Rebecca J. 6
"   Wm. N. 5
Wells, Wm. T. 2
West, Carson R. 3

West, Marilla 1
Westmoreland, Jerome W. 9
    "   Jesse 2(2)
White, B.W. 4
  "   Elijah 9
  "   Elizabeth 6
  "   James 1
  "   J.K. 2
  "   Jos. E. 9
  "   Mary 2
  "   Mary F. 5
Whitfield, Copeland 3
  "   Mary J. 2
Whitt, Ephriam D. 2
  "   Isaac 2
Whitten, J.W. 9
Wilkerson, Mary E. 7
Wilk(e)s, John S. 7
  "   Leroy W. 8
  "   Wm. H. 5
Williams, Geo. W. 10
  "   John S. 7,8,11
  "   Martha 8
  "   Mary E. 10
  "   Robert 2
  "   Willoughby 11
Williamson, Martha R. 10
Wilsford, Zella R. 5

Wilson, Andrew W. 3
  "   Boon 6
  "   Louisa M. 2
  "   Sarah A. 2
Winn, Minor H. 2
Wisdon, Leander 6
Witt, Carter H. 8
Woldridge, Andrew J. 6
  "   Elizabeth 6
Woodard, Hiram C. 11
Wood(s), Jane E. 2
  "   John M. 10
  "   Wm. 5
Woodson, Wm. P. 7
Woodward, Elizabeth 2
Wright, Newton E. 1
  "   William 5

Yarbrough, David 2
Young, Joseph 5,8
Young, Mary E. 11